Jam Session

Sammy Sosa

Terri Dougherty
ABDO Publishing Company

visit us at
www.abdopub.com

Published by ABDO Publishing Company, 4940 Viking Drive, Suite 622, Edina, Minnesota 55435.
Copyright © 1999 by Abdo Consulting Group, Inc. International copyrights reserved in all countries. No part of this book may be reproduced in any form without written permission from the publisher.

Printed in the United States.

Cover and Interior Photo credits: AP/Wide World Photos

Edited by Denis Dougherty

Sources: Associated Press; Chicago Tribune; New York Daily News; Sports Illustrated; Sports Illustrated For Kids; Time Magazine; Washington Post

Library of Congress Cataloging-in-Publication Data

Dougherty, Terri.
    Sammy Sosa / Terri Dougherty.
       p. cm. -- (Jam Session)
    Includes index.
    Summary: Presents the life and baseball career of Sammy Sosa, who, along with Mark McGwire, in 1998 broke the long-standing record of most home runs hit in a season.
    ISBN 1-57765-348-3 (hardcover)
    ISBN 1-57765-346-7 (paperback)
    1. Sosa, Sammy 1968- --Juvenile literature.   2. Baseball players--Dominican Republic--Biography--Juvenile literature. [1. Sosa, Sammy, 1968- . 2. Baseball players.]   I. Title.
II. Series.
GV865.S59D68   1999
796.357'092--dc21
   [B]   98-43185
                                                 CIP
                                                 AC

Contents

Slammin' Sammy

*I*n June 1998, home runs fell like rain for the Chicago Cubs' Sammy Sosa. "I've seen a lot of things in this game, but I've never seen anything like this," teammate Mark Grace said.

In the first 21 days of June, Sosa hit 17 home runs. With nine days left in the month, he had already broken the June home run record held by Babe Ruth, Bob Johnson, Roger Maris, and Pedro Guerrero.

When the month ended, Sammy had 20 home runs. That was two more than had ever been hit in a single month in Major League Baseball. The Detroit Tigers' Rudy York hit 18 in August 1937.

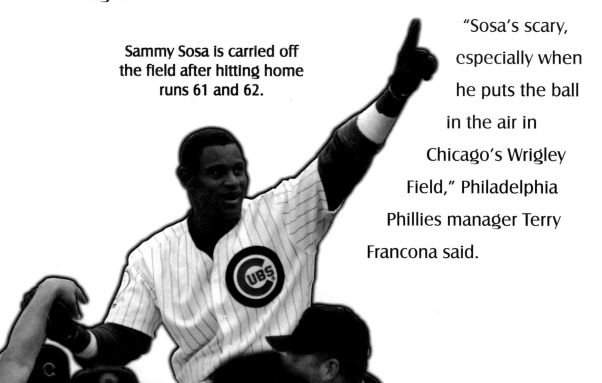

Sammy Sosa is carried off the field after hitting home runs 61 and 62.

"Sosa's scary, especially when he puts the ball in the air in Chicago's Wrigley Field," Philadelphia Phillies manager Terry Francona said.

Sammy's home run downpour was more than a brief cloudburst. It was the beginning of a remarkable summer for Sammy. He challenged the St. Louis Cardinals' Mark McGwire as both attempted to break Roger Maris' record of 61 home runs in a season, set in 1961.

Sammy was an unlikely contender for the home run record. In the past he had swung at bad pitches and struck out almost as often as he got a hit. But he had worked hard during the off-season to improve his swing, and was relaxed and patient at the plate.

"This is like a sample," Sammy said. "To show the people what kind of person I am. To show the people I am there. And I'm going to be there for them."

Sammy watches his 62nd home run go over the fence against the Milwaukee Brewers on September 13, 1998.

Humble Beginnings

When Sammy was growing up in San Pedro de Macoris in the Dominican Republic, he didn't dream of breaking Maris' home run record. He didn't even know who the former New York Yankees slugger was. Baseball heroes were far removed from the poor streets where he grew up.

"I never was a fan," Sammy once said. "I didn't know who this guy was or that guy was. I was busy working, trying to make money for my mother because she was struggling when my father died."

Sammy was born November 12, 1968, and his father died when Sammy was seven. To help support his family, Sammy sold oranges for 10 cents and shined shoes for 25 cents.

He was the fifth of seven children. He lived with his four brothers and two sisters in a two-room apartment in what was once a hospital. He slept on a thin mattress on the floor, and was often hungry.

"Only I know what I went through when I was struggling," Sammy said. "Now when I look at everything, it makes me feel good, it makes me feel proud of myself."

Boys play baseball in the streets of San Pedro de Macoris, Dominican Republic–Sammy Sosa's hometown.

From the Ring to the Diamond

When Sammy was 14, his brother suggested he try playing organized baseball. Sammy was already into sports, and was a boxer, but his mother didn't like seeing him get hit.

"He told me, 'It's nothing,' " his mother, Lucrecia, said. "I told him, 'My son, for a mother it's a lot.' "

So Sammy turned from the ring to the diamond. He and his brother practiced in sugarcane fields. Real baseball equipment was scarce. Sammy batted with a tree branch, used a rolled-up sock for a baseball, and turned a milk carton into a glove. He played whenever he could.

"The only way I could take care of my mother was to come to the major leagues and try to make it," Sammy said. "I would say to my mother, 'Don't worry about it, I'm going to take care of you.' "

Sammy loved baseball, but he also had to work at a shoe factory to help support his family. He decided to leave high school to concentrate on his sport.

"He told me, 'Mami, I can't study and play at the same time,' " his mother said. "He insisted. He said, 'I have to make it, Mami. I have to make it.' And I never doubted him."

In 1985, when he was 16, Sammy was invited to a tryout by major league scout Omar Minaya of the Texas Rangers. He had to ride a bus for four hours to get from a camp run by the Toronto Blue Jays in Santo Domingo to the tryout in Puerta Plata.

Sammy was thin, his spikes had a hole in them, and he had to borrow an old red jersey that had holes in it, too. But he impressed Minaya. He was aggressive on the field and the ball popped off his bat.

Sammy Sosa (center) on the field with the Texas Rangers.

"This is where the Sammy Sosa miracle began," Minaya said. "He got off the bus ready to hit. There was something inside him, a fire. Right from the start, you could see how aggressive he was."

Sammy wasn't a disciplined player, however, and it showed. He had a powerful arm, but he couldn't control his throws. His rockets from right field would sometimes fly right past the catcher into the stands.

Still, Minaya saw promise in Sammy and came to the Sosa home to give Sammy his first baseball paycheck for $3,500. Sammy gave almost all of it to his mother, but used some to buy his first bicycle.

Sammy barely beats the ball to second base as he makes a great steal while playing for the Chicago White Sox.

Growing Pains

Sammy began his baseball career in the United States in the Gulf Coast Rookie League in 1986. He led the league in doubles and total bases. After spending three years in the minor leagues, he was called up to the majors by the Rangers. He hit his first major league home run that year, off Boston Red Sox great Roger Clemens.

He was traded to the Chicago White Sox in the middle of the 1989 season. In 1990, his first full season in the majors, he batted only .233, but was the only American League player to reach double figures in doubles, triples, home runs, and steals.

He hit two home runs on opening day in 1991, but struggled at the plate after that. He ended the season batting .203 and spent part of the year back in the minor leagues.

The next season, Sammy became a Cub. "When he first got here, you could see he had great physical skills, but he was so raw," Grace, the Cubs' star first baseman, said. "He didn't know how to play the game. He didn't understand the concept of hitting behind runners. He didn't understand the concept of hitting the cutoff man to keep a double play in order. So many little things he just didn't know."

Sammy had a long way to go to polish his talent, but he felt at home with the Cubs. "I started feeling more comfortable when I got here," Sammy said. "I felt I had more of an opportunity here because they traded me here to play me every day."

Even though he made mistakes, Sammy showed he was a powerful hitter and aggressive base runner. In 1993, he became the first Cubs player to hit at least 30 home runs and steal at least 30 bases in a season. He was so proud of his accomplishment he had a large gold and diamond pendant made with the numbers 30-30 on it.

Sammy was named to the All-Star team in 1995, when he again made the 30-30 club. Sammy went on a home run tear the next season. He had 40 home runs and 100 runs batted in by August 20, when he was hit by a pitch. His hand was broken, and his season was over.

Sammy showed great potential, but his talent was still often untamed. He made many mistakes, sometimes throwing the ball to the wrong base. The fans in the Wrigley Field right field

Sammy makes a leaping catch in right field.

bleachers would chant, "How many outs, Sammy?" to make sure he was keeping his mind in the game. Sammy would good-naturedly hold up one or two fingers to show he was keeping track.

Sammy blasts another homer!

Cubs Show Sammy the Money

During spring training in 1997, Sammy was asked if he thought he could hit 50 home runs that year. "Why not 60?" Sammy replied. He didn't get close to the record that season, hitting 36 home runs. He was not patient at the plate and often swung at bad pitches. He struck out 174 times, the most of anyone in the National League that season.

He tried so hard to repeat his 30-steal, 30-home run performance that he was too reckless on the basepaths, and ended the season with 22 steals in 34 attempts. His manager, Jim Riggleman, had to scold him in the dugout for his foolish base running.

"I was trying to do too much," Sammy said. "I'd go to the plate with no idea and swing at everything." Sammy swung and ran with abandon because he thought he needed impressive statistics to make money to support his mother and family.

"It's not easy for a Latin player to take 100 walks," Sammy said the next season. "If I knew the stuff I know now seven years ago—taking pitches, being more relaxed, I would have put up even better numbers. But people have to understand where you're coming from."

Even though he made mistakes, the Cubs believed in Sammy. They signed him to a four year, $42.5 million contract during the middle of the 1997 season. "The one important variable was Sammy's maturity as a player," Cubs general manager Ed Lynch said. "We were banking that he would continue to improve."

The new contract put Sammy's mind at ease. "There was too much pressure last year," Sammy said in 1998. "I was trying to hit two home runs in one at-bat. Now I don't feel that anymore."

Sammy Sosa slides safely into third base.

Sammy Sizzles

*D*uring spring training in 1998, much of the talk centered on the possibility that Maris' record of 61 home runs in a season would fall. McGwire and Seattle's Ken Griffey Jr. were mentioned frequently as potential record-breakers, but not Sammy.

Sammy, however, had worked hard during the off-season to improve. He watched a tape put together by Cubs hitting coach Jeff Pentland. "I want to hit .300," he told Pentland. Sammy entered the 1998 season as a career .257 hitter.

Before home games in '98, Sammy worked with Pentland. Before batting practice they would go to the batting tunnel under the right field bleachers at Wrigley Field. Sammy worked on being patient at the plate, and not going after bad pitches.

"That's the big thing for all good hitters. They don't swing at bad balls, and they hammer mistakes," Phillies catcher Mark Parent said. "They make you pay for every mistake. That's what Sammy's doing."

Sammy entered the Great Home Run Race of '98 with a bang. Between May 25 and June 21 he hit 21 home runs in 22 games. Sammy's hot bat was also helping the Cubs have their best season of the 1990s. They were in contention for a wild-card playoff berth in the National League. Cubs fans in the right field bleachers yelled, "M-V-P! M-V-P!"

Sammy wasn't as concerned with his home run pace as he was with the Cubs' chances of making the playoffs. When he was asked about the possibility of hitting more home runs than Babe Ruth (60 in a 154-game schedule in 1927) or Maris had in a single season, he said, "I don't want you to put me in that kind of company."

"Now I think he knows there's nothing like having a good season and winning," Grace said.

Sammy takes a huge cut.

Smiling Slugger

*E*ven though he downplayed his chances to set a home run record, Sammy enjoyed the attention that came with the home run chase. He was having fun.

"Pressure? Pressure for me was when I was back home in the Dominican, trying to make it to the major leagues. That was pressure for me. Right now, I don't see pressure on me. I never know what pressure means," Sammy said.

"He just loves what he's doing," teammate Gary Gaetti said. "He doesn't make a big deal out of it. He just goes about his business and he's worked very hard to get where he is with all that time in the (batting) cage."

Sammy's humor won over many fans across the country during the home run chase. His one-liners often caused reporters, who crowded around his locker before and after games, to break out in laughter.

Sammy entertains reporters before a game.

When asked the name of his first love, Sammy replied: "Cartoons." When McGwire said he looked forward to seeing Ruth and Maris in heaven, Sammy quipped: "Don't forget about me."

Sammy would sprint to his position in right field, waving to fans in the bleachers at Wrigley. He had a smile on his face every day. "I have a good time and I'm ready for (interviews and autograph requests) everywhere that I go, because I'm having the best season of my life," Sammy said.

After each home run, Sammy blew his famous two-fingered kiss to his mother, who would be watching the game on TV in the house Sammy bought for her. "It is like I'm being hugged," she said. "He's very sweet."

Sammy acknowledges his mother, who watches his games on TV in the Dominican Republic.

"He's had a very humble upbringing, but a proud upbringing," Riggleman said. "He's very dedicated to his family in the Dominican. He has a sense of peace about him that he knows he's making them proud when he goes out there."

Chicago Cubs slugger Sammy Sosa signs autographs for fans before a game.

Sosa benefited from having the great hitting of Grace and Henry Rodriguez protecting him in the lineup. He saw many good pitches, and took advantage. In addition to hitting home runs at a record pace, he also led the National League in runs batted in.

"In June, when he broke the home run record, he didn't get any intentional walks," Grace said. "He came to me and thanked me. He's very humble, a great teammate."

The Chase Heats Up

Sammy led the home run chase briefly for the first time, when he hit his 48th on August 19 in Wrigley Field against McGwire and the Cardinals. But he didn't hold the lead long. McGwire hit two later in the same game, bringing his total to 49.

On September 2, Sammy broke Hack Wilson's Cubs record of 56 home runs in a season, set in 1930. The fan who caught the ball wanted to give it back to Sammy, but he signed it and returned it to the fan. "You give it to me, I give it to you," Sammy said.

Sammy had fun as he chased Maris' record, but he didn't expect to break it first. He gave that nod to McGwire, calling him "The Man." After McGwire hit his 59th, Sammy predicted the Cardinals first baseman would shatter Maris' mark.

"Seventy, he can do it," Sammy said. "He's Superman. Everybody knows I'm pulling for Mark, I just want to make the playoffs and if that happens, the whole season will be better. I just love what is happening."

When McGwire tied Maris' record on September 7, Sammy joined the crowd in applauding the feat. When Sammy singled in the eighth inning, he hugged McGwire at first base. And when

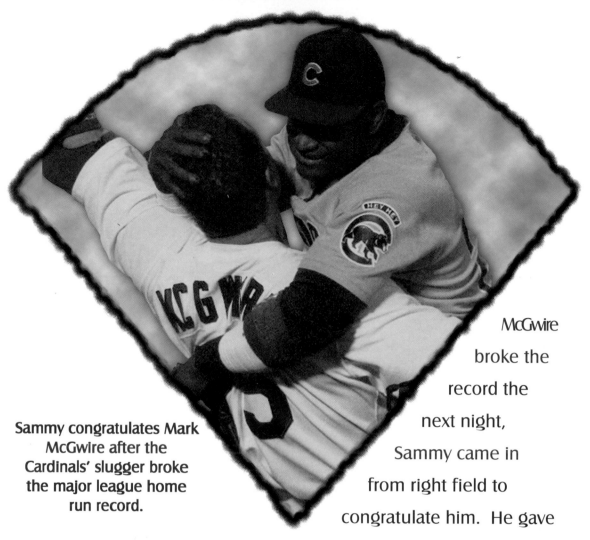

Sammy congratulates Mark McGwire after the Cardinals' slugger broke the major league home run record.

McGwire broke the record the next night, Sammy came in from right field to congratulate him. He gave McGwire an emotional hug near the Cardinals' dugout.

"I told him 'Maybe now you can go to your house and relax and take it easy,'" Sammy said. "He was real proud of himself and happy and said 'Unbelievable. I don't know what was happening out there.' I said, 'You did it. That's why you're The Man.' "

McGwire had praised Sammy all season, once saying "He's having a much better year than me." After he broke the record, McGwire showed his respect for his friendly foe when he said: "To all my family, my son, the Cubs, Sammy Sosa. It's unbelievable."

Sosa shattered Roger Maris' record of 61 home runs in a single season by smashing 66.

Dominican Hero

Sammy's hitting had a lot to do with the Cubs making the playoffs in 1998. "I have a job to do and I want to contribute in every way to get Chicago into the playoffs and the World Series," Sammy said. "It's not just home runs."

Although McGwire got most of the attention in America during the home run chase, Sammy was the hero in his native country. "He is 'The Man' in the United States. I am 'The Man' in the Dominican Republic," Sammy said.

"We are very proud of his performance," said Franklyn Mirabel, sports editor of Santo Domingo's Hoy newspaper. "When a guy like him makes it, it's very important for our country."

The Dominican Republic Sports Ministry presents the Florida Marlins' Jesus Sanchez, second from left, and the Chicago Cubs' Sammy Sosa, third from left, with awards for being sports goodwill ambassadors.

Sammy is a hero to his home country off the field as well. When the Dominican Republic was hit hard by Hurricane Georges toward the end of the 1998 season, Sammy helped by donating food and supplies. Sammy also built a shopping mall there. "This isn't about baseball history," Sammy said. "This is about people in my country who don't have anything."

McGwire topped Sammy in the Great Home Run Race of '98, 70 to 66. But Sammy had an MVP season and led his Cubs to the playoffs. Although the Cubs lost in the first round, Sammy became a true hero to people all over the world.

Sammy is thankful to have the opportunity to play the game he loves. "God bless America," he said. "I love this country. Whatever happens to me now, I think it's a gift. Every day is a holiday for me. My life is kind of like a miracle."

Dominicans cheer for Sammy as he hits home run number 62.

Sammy Sosa Profile

Born: Nov. 12, 1968, in San Pedro de Macoris, Dominican Republic

Height: 6 feet

Weight: 200 pounds

Position: Right Field

Bats: Right

Throws: Right

Honors

National League Player of the Week,
1993, 1995 (twice), 1996, 1997,
1998 (three times)

National League Player of the Month,
July 1996, June 1998

Silver Slugger Award, 1995

National League All-Star, 1995, 1998

National League MVP, 1998

Chronology

November 12, 1968 - Sammy Sosa is born in San Pedro de Macoris, Dominican Republic.

July 30, 1985 - Signed as a non-drafted free agent by the Texas Rangers.

1986 - Makes his professional baseball debut in the Gulf Coast Rookie League. Leads the league in doubles, with 19, and total bases, with 96.

1987 - A midseason all-star in the South Atlantic League.

1988 - Leads the Florida State League with 12 triples, steals a career-high 42 bases.

June 16, 1989 - Makes major league debut with the Texas Rangers.

July 29, 1989 - Traded to the Chicago White Sox.

1990 - Plays first full major league season. Only American League player to reach double figures in doubles (26), triples (10), home runs (15), and steals (32).

March 30, 1992 - Traded to the Chicago Cubs for George Bell.

1993 - Becomes first Cubs player to hit 30 home runs and steal 30 bases in a season. Finishes season with 33 home runs and 36 stolen bases.

1995 - Hits 36 home runs, steals 34 bases, and has 119 RBI. Named to *The Sporting News* National League All-Star Team.

July 11, 1995 - Plays in first All-Star Game.

May 16, 1996 - Becomes first player in Cubs history to hit two home runs in an inning.

August 20, 1996 - Season ends when he's hit by a pitch and injured. Ends the year with 40 home runs and 100 RBI.

1997 - Equals career high with 119 RBI.

1998 - Hits 20 home runs in June, the most of any player in any month in major league history. Finishes with 66 home runs and a .308 batting average. Sosa is named the National League MVP.

September 13, 1998 - Hits two home runs in a game against the Milwaukee Brewers to give him 62 home runs for the season. Sammy, along with Mark McGwire, breaks the 37-year-old home run record set by Roger Maris.

Major League Batting Average

1989	Rangers/White Sox	.255
1990	White Sox	.233
1991	White Sox	.203
1992	Cubs	.260
1993	Cubs	.261
1994	Cubs	.300
1995	Cubs	.268
1996	Cubs	.273
1997	Cubs	.251
1998	Cubs	.308

Sosa hits another one out of Wrigley Field.

Major League Home Runs

1989	Rangers/White Sox	4
1990	White Sox	15
1991	White Sox	10
1992	Cubs	8
1993	Cubs	33
1994	Cubs	25
1995	Cubs	36
1996	Cubs	40
1997	Cubs	36
1998	Cubs	66

Sosa rounds the bases after hitting number 65 in Milwaukee on September 23, 1998.

Glossary

CUTOFF MAN - A player, usually an infielder, who catches a throw from the outfield and decides where to make the play.

DOMINICAN REPUBLIC - A country of 18,816 square miles in the eastern part of the island of Hispaniola, in the West Indies. Its capital is Santo Domingo.

DOUBLE PLAY - To make two outs on one play.

HOME RUN - A ball hit far enough that the batter touches all the bases and scores a run.

MAJOR LEAGUE - The top league in a professional sport. In baseball, the clubs in the American League and National League are in the major leagues.

MINOR LEAGUE - A group of professional organized teams playing against each other in a league below the major leagues.

PLAYOFFS - Games played by division winners and wild-card teams after the regular season.

RECORD - The best performance.

SPIKES - Shoes, used for playing baseball, that have sharp points on the soles and often on the heels to prevent the wearer from slipping.

STRIKE - To swing at a ball and miss, or to not swing at a ball in the strike zone. A ball hit foul but not caught is also a strike when the batter has less than two strikes.

STRIKE OUT - To make an out in baseball with three strikes.

Index